conjuring the dead

kumani

WordHouse Books is an imprint of
the Baltimore Writers' Alliance,
dedicated to promoting
the literary arts in Maryland.
Send correspondence to
P.O. Box 6240, Baltimore, MD 21206.

Publisher's Cataloging-in-Publication
(Provided by Quality Books, Inc.)

Kumani
    Conjuring the dead / by Kumani
    p. cm.
    ISBN 1-891529-10-2

    1. Death–Poetry.  I. Title.

PS3611.U636C66 2003      811'.6
                       QBI33-1499

Cover artwork "Freda"- detail,
by Sam Christian Holmes

*Copyright ©2003 by Denise Gantt.*
*Published in the United States by WordHouse Books.*
ALL RIGHTS RESERVED

*For Rebecca Rice*
*(1947-2002)*

# Contents

Foreword

*Part I: The Egungun*

    Psalm for an Impending Rapture     3

    Sight     4

    Ayofemi     8

    Seeing God     9

    For Virginia     10

    The Sacred Bread     12

    The Cup     16

    After...     17

    The Blues     19

    Sugarcane     20

    Alisha     21

    Angels     23

    Annie Frye     25

    Integration Part One     27

    A Coil Called Skin     28

    Integration Part Two     31

*Part II: Burning Karma*

| | |
|---|---|
| Ulysses | 35 |
| Tears for Yashodhara | 37 |
| Dionysus' Child | 38 |
| Waking to Wound | 40 |
| the pickup | 41 |
| Drinking Coffee | 43 |
| Requiem | 45 |
| Poem for a Black Man I Once Loved | 48 |
| Mandala | 50 |
| moonkissed | 52 |
| The Glance | 53 |
| Burning Karma | 55 |
| what a smooth Taoist brother intimated before kissing | 56 |
| Coda | 58 |
| Stillness/September 10, 2001 | 59 |
| Passport for the Recently Dead | 60 |

# Foreword: In the Visible Light

*conjuring the dead* witnesses the poet's sojourn within the dimensions of language, a sojourn to explore the complexity of self made manifest by history and suffering. It is the gaze upon the self, not unlike the gaze of the negritude poets onto their postcolonial landscapes. Kumani is one of a number of younger contemporary voices who look beyond African origins for other cultural clues first to a wholeness of self and in that way discover a wholeness of culture. *conjuring the dead* is the heart touching humanity with a new vulnerability, a willingness to extend beyond the familiar. The descent into the wreckage of a history is here distinctly feminine, even as the poet finds the descent leaves her self still woven into a befuddling present. Kumani finds an assemblage of discordant notes in the space of present time, which she uses to write a festive song and rename love, beyond suffering and difference to an acceptance, full as it is with nuance.

In "A Coil Called Skin," she writes, "...in that coil called skin, /there is a memory before chains. /But I cannot conjure it." The book names and conjures, working a ritualistic frenzy in lines driven by feeling. In the end Kumani names and claims her heart as her own. "The Glance" touches this frenzy. "Oh, I am ruined now. Happy day."

In her first book, a poet works to establish her own language, to know the local tongue and its place in the context of the whole of that language, to search her feelings about what she imagines comprises her experience, and to sort through the universe of construction to find the line and the organization she can claim, claim and use to build her poetic project. That poetic project is a landscape of one's own senses, and the first book is her announcement of an intention to live there, to know, over the span of a life, what it means to see one's heart manifest itself as a landscape, one larger than an actual heart but smaller than the space inside her that contains thought. It is thought that is the breath of poetry, the atmosphere of a landscape called a poet's life project.

Blending elements of the African with references from the Yoruba and the Asian with references from Buddhism and Daoism, Kumani acknowledges pain and joy, keeping to a fragile balance. The first half of the book is entitled "The Egungun," the Yoruba term for ancestors, and here she searches the past for signs of recognition. The awareness of a collective past should free us as individuals, but the poet more honestly admits a deeper terror, namely that of recognizing the past as too vast a place, too incomprehensible a complex of signs, and too human an experience to neatly validate identities we carve out of the exigencies of today or tomorrow.

Early in the first section, "The Sacred Bread" traces the history of African women along the lines of bread as communal ritual and bonding. Kumani looks to God and sees Her moving through, as one would make bread. The observations of the poet do not shy away from the harsher perceptions. "For even in stories as ancient as Eve/we are still bound and gagged." The lines in these poems are open and extended, not for the maternal reception but for the arcing sweep of wings spread over an awesome length, circumnavigating a history of pain. In the end, she turns a Buddhist nod to all this difficult processing. "Yes, I whisper.../ let the cup of water/ quiver against love's relentless dance./ I am a sweeter sacrament because of you."

"Burning Karma," the second section of this collection, breathes a Daoist breath for questioning and acceptance, full of courage and unsure of the landing. The poet knows there is no surety in searching the self, searching with the knowledge that self must be abandoned, that one must relinquish the Lacanian mirror with all its anxieties. To that end she seeks both emptiness and fullness, as the two modulate inside a psyche burgeoning with history and culture. The weaving takes on complex textures. In "Dionysus' Child," Kumani works the Greco-Roman with the Nigerian, naming her goddess Oshun, the Yoruba orisha who presides over creativity and childbirth and is representative of the entire feminine manifestation. The poet asks of celestial entities, "Don't you remember..?"

*conjuring the dead* is cause for celebration. These are poems that sing against the limits of voice, taking on the affairs of the human heart from one heart aimed steadily at a complex serenity, one not resigned to the difficulties of compassion and love or to the fear of injustice and suffering. Most importantly, they arise from a knowledge of the craft of the business of being a poet. Langston Hughes' "Twelve Moods for Jazz" echoes here in the registers with Adrienne Rich's "Diving into the Wreck" in lines that know the longer expression of the Beats as well as Rita Dove's *Thomas and Beulah* with its compression. In this first collection, Kumani has granted herself the artistic license to be brave, to carve words out of the petrified skin of wounds so horrible that they have been denied their own song, until voices like this one arrive and anxiously relieve those silences. Selah!

Afaa Michael Weaver
aka Wei Yafeng
Simmons College
Boston, Massachusetts
June 28, 2003

*Part 1: The Egungun*

# Psalm for an Impending Rapture

### for Erika & Rebecca

When we finally tumble to earth —
stretched haphazardly
from heavenly places,
it is the motion, not the light
which requires us to breathe.

Involuntarily, yet with care
we conspire to you love.
Our tiny lungs meet the morning with mere survival.

*The parting stains sweet . . . .*

I do not recall when I staggered from god's grace to yours,
but I am held inside the walls of many countries,
carved by many wombs.
In a room shaped by placenta, I gather my weapons,
ready to make war no more,

and conspire . . . .

On the battlefield,
a prism of dark hands comes to greet me, and
we strain to make language, but there
is little choice now.

Against the abyss of our tarnished armaments
I breathe you in.

Endure.

# Sight

I. *Daylight*

Today my mind is a wound,
it secretly writhes in the garden,
sucking fruit, suffocating light —
like a worm.

I thumb through books,
nightmared and ruined,
I thumb through —
and the same voices come
crashing through my Bible and Gita,
christening floodgates with cinders,
and easy fantasies of love.

Imagine sitting with Gandhi,
defiant smiles staring down the barrel
of a shotgun, sun-bleached bones
draped in sackcloth, plucking tears of women
stoned for their brother's sins,
their ashes resurrected into Devi,
with wide arms full of children
suckling never emptied breasts,
their knotty heads combed with sacred grit and science.

In the vision
I float above my body's name,
neither redwood nor garnet,
flesh nor spirit, woman nor goddess.
Something different.

*But not today.*

Today, there is a phantom burning in my chest.
It shovels my head.
I, a gentle woman,
born from the ancestors of slaves,
my *Egungun* screaming.

Tonight they beckon, *tell them how much we suffered.*
I oblige then pray for a slave named Sarah —
her man/dead/baby/sold.

Against the hands of Polaris,
feel a noose around my neck,
bend on solid ground and
beseech heaven for different sight,
these corneas fixated on the dead like a habit,
as I light the white candle,
water the rose of Jericho,
pray to four directions,
then ask the *Egungun* to sit,
my head achy
as a multitude of ghosts moan *write it down.*

With throbbing temples understand why Oedipus gouged his sight.

Perhaps truth nothing more than an unthinkable shadow
every soul must see.


II. *The Vision*

Sleep comes on me like a fit, its dream heavy.
Nestled in sweat, I float to my kin,
a circle of stone faces huddled near
Massa Perkins' place, Athens, Georgia 1849.
Nomads wandering earth unable to find heaven,
their veins full of brittle memory —
an iron collar rusting 'round their necks,
for a bit of fat meat stolen,
or a cup of flour hidden from the mealy worms
underneath the floorboards in the quarter.

*Somebody calls me Viney*
*and I respond.*

A man named Titus cups his raw fingers into mine,
whispers: *these are some hard times, slavery days.*
*Watched 'em kill my pa, beat my mammy,*
*climb into every one of my sisters,*
*sell my children 'way.*
*Stood me on the auction block,*
*stripped me down naked*
*negotiatin' a price.*

His one huge tear nearly puts out the fire.

Like the blind, I touch his face,
skin wrinkled where lines are never cast.
Ask him: *why you never leave this place,*
and he say, *I'm still looking for my babies.*
*Remember them bright as summer,*
*Lucindy May and Mary Tamsie.*
*Blue black like Lue.*
*I reckons if I find 'em, I'll be released.*

The drawstring of his tattered shirt loosens,
slips down the seams of his shoulders, revealing
a back full of odd scars raised fat from a whip,
blistered, then crisscrossed.
My hands trace the disfigurement for recognition
but I don't ask him no more questions.

Slowly, a woman moves toward us,
draws a set of bones from her apron,
she is in the middle of life,
her face transfixed in neither frown nor prayer.

Black eyes, no pupils,
stare hard at them bones
shaved down to unworldly ecru.
The woman mutters an odd language,
then holds them out for all to see.

The people moan
as those pieces of bone linger unnaturally long
in the midnight air, their message
heated by dreams of freedom
and Massa Perkins' hounds.
Prophecy speaking truth in the low grass.

Then that conjure woman
full of spirits turns those shadow eyes
on me —
*remember how much we suffered,*
*how our blood still soaks the roots of Golgotha,*
*and we done put a curse upon this land*
*for the memory of slaves never die.*

Slowly, my kin fade to specter,
and the ghost land drifts to dreamtime
as the woman places those sight-filled bones
in my once innocent hands.

Upon waking,
I rub and rub and rub
just like Pilate,
but nothing will remove the stain.

# Ayofemi

Somewhere in a dark water
a Yoruba woman wails. 1697.
She can no longer remember
the color of stars
the feeling of rain
most days she cannot recollect
her feelings
ankles shackled
hands loose
as a foreign tongue urges stillness.

The woman cannot understand
but is sure of his man/speech
sure she will not bear this devil's touch again
as she recites her name, pupils stained
by the whiteness bloodying her thighs.

With each fondle she vengefully imagines
laying out the palm butter for *Ellegbara (god of the crossroads)*,
dancing hauntingly to the rhythm of the *djembe (the drum)*
before all is loss, she dreams of snuggling close
to her *babba (her father)*, the ripe sacrifice of mangoes and
pounded yam moistening the Orisha's lips *(ebos)*,
she summons forth the mysteries of the earth,
calls on *Oya (the goddess of the graveyard)*,
then on the *Egungun (the dead)*
and as if to pour acid into her captor's eyes,
she repeats her name over and over again,
like a mantra, like a prayer, until this
too is stolen, and she is laid to rest
inside Yemeya, mother of the world.

The ocean swollen
from the weight of all her
still/born.

# Seeing God

Today, I settle on this spark —
there can be no muddle or kiss without you.

Time twists to full stop, then quietly quakes to cloud water.

I see you god.     But flesh is fleeting.

Then, like the junkie unable to find her fix,
I claw at the same wound where you planted ecstasy,
tap the vein, find no solace, as I falsely name you judge.

Once, I followed a rainbow for miles, determined to find its end.
When I turned to check the mirror, it was gone
I drove, nearly hysterical trying to find that perfect prism,
instead of seeing your hearty grin stealing all that color from sky.

# For Virginia

I. *Words*

When I first heard your language,
let it flow out my mouth in Kate's play,
I was old.

Their declarations could have been
easily wasted on my youth,
like all those feeble promises I made to boys
with pinky swears.

But instead, they came
during my inferno
when I was in need of a poultice,
true and woman-filled.

Words flaming to lip like hand to offering,
kissing disappointment
with forgivable prayer.

It was then, that you reached from your nestled crook
and scrolled each line,
the labyrinths and gardens, kidney pie,
and rose-filled parties
with that immense ache and naming,
language painted to soul like skin,
familiar in our kinship. Sisters.
I, the woman who most certainly
would have served you in the kitchen with dismay.

When I was young
hieroglyphics etched the sky with wonder.
Now they fit me like prophecy,
in this search for madness and meaning.

II. *Dying*

Death takes many shapes —
I've seen a few. I saw its mask
flirt with a friend's face once.
No prayer would shake its veil from her anchor.

Since her passing, I have watched my gaze harden,
glow with the night-edge of woman,
things simple in Death's fragrance —
until even the flimsiest of visions
overwhelms.

Now the reaper sits on my bed every night.
We are old friends,
her frame identical
down to the butterfly birthmark on my back.

She knows everything,
impatient sentinel demanding
*what have you done,*
as I fight to live the life once promised.

No rocks weighing pockets down to moss-filled water,
though I call the river often,
its sturdy ramparts full of ink
and swell, dreams so sweet
they might even make the young boys swoon again
and release me from this spinster's web, Virginia,
as I search for that perfect phrase,
and *yes* is all I utter.

# The Sacred Bread

## for Rebecca

*Look: I feel how I'm moving away,*
*how I'm shedding my old life, leaf by leaf.*
*Only your smile spreads like sheer stars*
*over you and, soon now, over me.*
       *Rainer Maria Rilke*

It has been years since I baked the bread,
felt the hallowed kiss of simple things.
Wanting now to make myself a soft center
that holds all the good things to eat.

I peer from the steamed windows of my kitchen,
the glass staining a mesmerizing yes,
glance the full bloom of love's redemption.
Rilke, my kindred, stretches words of sacrifice
across the orange sky,
and I stand taller now, unable to recognize the face
that shines back from the paned glass.
So much more than this reflection.

My feast nearly ready.

In the light's descent, I hear you weeping.
A deep song, a woman's song.
Your frame a flutter of wings clashing green,
hair, a blaze of tangles,
the moon dances seductively by your feet,
as you greet me, eyes filled with regret,
the cancer woman appearing at sunset,
wailing against the sorrows of this women's grail —
of giving too much, not enough left over,
to carve your own dreams to the bone.

My older sister, who cradled my first words as manna,
sent roses when my heart began to fail,
appear, now, like Rebekah in Genesis,
dip your hands into the cool well water,
with lovely eyes invite me to drink,
a wandering Bodhisattva

reworking the pattern
to identify the wound.

In the kitchen, like the light diminished,
we fade against the bamboo shades.
Remember all the bread we will not bake, together.

The sun, like our love, settles inside the earth,
transforming you into a fury,
me into a mere mortal dissatisfied,
neither one of us grand enough to divert Death's kiss,
that uncompromising teacher,
who has made all our battles so insignificant and small.

Instead of tears, I begin to make the bread,
press my hands against the swirl of honey and yeast,
the cream and lavender pot sparkling fragile
against the warm     womb     water.

As the kitchen fills with the scent of sweet things and life.
I ache for you.    I long.

II.

*. . . and then he assigns you to his sacred fire that you may become sacred bread for God's sacred feast. All these things shall love do unto you.*
Kahlil Gibran

I add the flour in handfuls, mix in wheat and white.
The salt I shake,
take the knotted, rippled dough,
lay it on the marble slab, my hands,
not dissimilar to god's, knead.

My hands press, again and up and over,
again and up and down.
There in the hollow of the kitchen, together,
the yeast, the flour, the honey, the water,
your memory, my hands, bring forth the miracle,
the dough first a fist, now a round, full ball.

It is almost night.
A final hymn to day shakes the light down,
as I place the dough in a smooth bowl,
lay a wet towel against its shoulders.

In the stars' random motion I see god,
in the dough, mold life, like an expectant mother,
anticipate the baby's next kick,
my body a dark temple where life resides,
belly thick, pushing the damp cloth closer to heaven.

Again and again, I push, I knead, I repeat this pattern,
as god, unwavering, repeats her plan.
Exhausted, knees on floor, I yield.
Place dough on coals, wood fire,
watch it pass through flame,
the biscuits and challah,
injera and flatbread
all a memory of love's combustion.

Like the bread that is baking, I too am in preparation.
The steam from my windows drips coolness,
and I am as simple as condensation,
washed down like well water, essential, like bread, complete.
Astonished at how quickly a life flickers,
then flames —
to heat,
to fire,
to ash.

As I take the loaves from out the oven,
tap against their brown smooth shells,
you call from Cassiopeia's belly,
as beautiful as those nymphs that banished
our Ethiopian sister to a wretched grave.

*Why were we so foolish to believe their mythology?*

For even in stories as ancient as Eve
we are still bound and gagged. Obliterated.
The world, desperate in its search for truth,
unable to love its black mother.

The serrated knife cuts through the bread —
reveals something soft and mysterious within that familiar frame.
I remember our last meal together
sitting on the floor by your altar,
eating nan filled with spice,
laughing at our seriousness,
and how much we suffered for
this black/woman/skin.

Yes, I whisper,
as I lay out two plates of bread for us to eat,
light the pillar candle,
let the cup of water
quiver against love's relentless dance.

I am a sweeter sacrament because of you.

# The Cup

She beseeches, fill me,
glides her fingers through the gray mass,
wet clay glares hungrily from the center,

language a stranded chorus
disconnecting voice from heart,

messy hands a far better teacher.

From the wheel, the molded earth responds,
*I will yield from skin to river,*
*let nothing strangle it, I am the cup,*

and the woman cradles the rocky underbelly
scarred from babies and a lover's caverned pain.

Her wrinkled palms kindling the hard made vessel,
still covetous of its shape.

# After...

### for Maya

The sky is filled with earth-spun remnants,
dust,

the ancient web of Babel,
tears our tongues into splinters,

chaos paves a tattered road toward love,

*I grow dizzy....*

Like a greedy thief,
the rubble steals away all my childish metaphors,
my raw mouth sprouts truth,
I howl with wolves,
sit huddled on the futon,
until I am widdled into fear's coarse appendage.

The TV blinks,
and I half-believe I am special,
because Death did not wave her wand at me.

Later, the ghosts depart their ashen sepulcher,
float above the ground in ragged shoes.
They will wander for years huddled in my aorta,
my heart a repository for the dead.

Cradling my daughter,
I'll understand why a mourning father
might strap a bomb inside his shirt
and call me the enemy.

*Yesterday, 35,000 children died of starvation,*
*40 million people lived with AIDS,*
*and I continued to rotate on my axis.*

Near Chernobyl babies were born resembling Cyclops,
in Baltimore, black children died, as they do every day,
unnoticed, and as daylight sharpened new morning
there were people called untouchable,
as the world expired in two towers.

I surrender to a small and terrible knowing,
as the Fates weave their prophecy in every girl child's ear —
*if the women lose faith, all is lost.*

Wonder how long this lesson will last
before another building crumbles,
or a friend dies too quickly,
her soul a staggering arabesque toward heaven,
as a jealous lover bludgeons his wife,
or one more brother lays splattered against concrete on North & P —
the yellow police line stretching all the way to Sierra Leone,
where babies are slaughtered at the wrists
for that exquisite diamond a mother in Roland Park now sports,
as she takes up the knife, watches her white wrists turn to red,
like the wrists of dead black babies . . . .

How many more die
before we understand —
life, with no love,
has no meaning,
even with the cash.

# The Blues

## for Johnnett

Born from original folk and cacao,
I do not recall when I was begot by hatred's kiss,
black woman seeking salvation in an ancient jar of fade cream,
full, lined lips, never honored like brother's light eyes,
identity forever shackled to the bowels of a slave ship,
every corner of America spread firmly across my thighs.

Cheeks appear sullen, stained with a sad, yet undeniable hue.

Only now have I begun to see my mother's eyes in morning reflection.
Slowly, I learn to navigate their sorrows. Every day, I overcome,
my body round like my cousins'. Against a nappy head,
betray mammy with nightmares of white skin and golden tresses.
Poisoned and in recovery.

Spy us by the bus stop, in the corner aisles of supermarkets,
fingering sweets, our walls of flesh, acid tongues,
mechanisms for survival, never complaining for fear
Nanna will whip our sorry asses, or better yet, urge us to seek Jesus.
Even when we tell her white Jesus is a lie.

I do not remember when I learned to abuse you
like a strong and palpable liquor.
My blues are a junkie's rum.

No Nanna, I have never cut cane, but look,
my back is broken by less perceptible things.

Don't you see
my god is blue black,
her ample body streaking the sky indigo.

There she makes rain from a divine, yet bitter love.

# Sugarcane

Machetes cut and kill —
now imagine
if you were my crop.

Against the peach and pale of worn out sheets,
I chop you down,
my field of Canaan.
Wet with milky tears,
I hide underneath the shade of large,
bowed widows,
and streak my face with your liquor.

Soon I'll be like all the other nappy-headed girls —
a bushy triangle made of slavery, cane, and
of course the rum.

Drunk,
I imagine chewing
your cracked up pieces of bone
until the marrow fits neatly into my mouth.
Under the fine corners of breast,
I slaughter sugar like you butcher cane,
and never flinch at the gummy insides.

In the field,
you sharpen your tongue afraid
these Florida crystals might stain your cheeks.
But these hands were made for more than chopping
and I know what to do,

how to cut you down,
down boy,
*Massas comin' to the quarter tonight,*
*boys*
*slice me a piece*
and like the black, the
sweetness stains forever.

Now imagine if
you were my crop
and I was given the plow . . . .

# Alisha

When I am four I learn the truth —
it is not safe to be a little Black girl in America.
Hear the story of how four girls prayed,
then were killed inside God's temple.
When we go to Corinthian Baptist Church
I am always looking for a bomb.

Later, I learn this lesson deeper,
as they find your skin underneath huge bowed trees,
much like the ones our ancestors sought for shade.

I am an old woman at 21,
and you are my first homicide.

Now your ghost hunts the bare forest,
smooth, black skin graces memory,
hair slung to ponytail tight, dances.

I cry, but I am suspect of tears.

No sweet face, black, swallowed the TV,
when they found you dead 20 years ago
last seen at a library
where Black girls don't often circulate.

Last seen talking to a White man.

Then, as if to save the other women
they cut down the trees in front of campus,
but they aren't the extremities that killed you.

As I grow older,
your ghost scratches my bones.
I still see us sitting in Stimson dining hall,
your eyes with the dark pupils
urging me to pray. Then you whisper,
softly, as if God has allowed you
only one sound,

*all blood,* you say
*when it hits air,*
*turns from ruby to brown to black.*
*Why is some more red?*

# Angels

I am six.
I have stopped seeing angels
everywhere.

I use to see them all the time
until I realized everyone does
not have a heart made of second sight.
Now, I learn to be quiet,
even as their voices push the swing
and I can fly.

Now, they hide,
slip into corners,
mask their willowy clothes
against the wind,

as I watch TV,
the small black and white screen
sharing the same picture in-between
Lucille Ball, Opie, and Batman.

Bodies huddled outside a motel.
*Pointing. Someone dying. A black man.*

It is 1968, the summer of love.
I wear a paper dress and a peace sign to camp.
Get wet, watch the red pulped fabric turn to mush.

When my mother picks me up,
her eyes are the same centerpiece of disappointment
as when Martin died.

Later when I meet Angela Davis,
sit with her eating split peas and millet,
she will tell me, for some, the revolution was only fashion.

But at camp, in the summer of '68,
death counts scrolling every night on the CBS News,
and I innocently wonder why there are so many Viet Cong dead,
I fashion a different self.

Free and loud, singing kumbaya,
hammers and rainbows painted eternally on cheeks,
I watch a long trail of cars stream to a field,
everyone dances in mud.
Listen to Ritchie Havens and Crosby Stills and Nash.
Dirty dirty angels. Flying . . . .

I dream of packing Raggedy Ann
and finding young people with long hair to love me.
At camp I wear everyone's love beads.
I know god, see her drifting innocently
with the wood nymphs as we roast marshmallows.

Each day at the end of camp
we sit in a circle inside a hollow barn,
all those brown white tan black kids
know the secret handshake, but when we
grow old we forget the meaning of peace signs.

At YMCA we swim,
I so enjoy the feeling of my head
bobby underneath water.

Then, suddenly, as if a life-long caution to joy,
I quickly learn what it means to be a girl, ripe, stolen.
Heart thoughts ripple inside my tense skin,
and the child born with the bald spots
disappears into the back of her head.

I do not remember what young man
rewrote my privates.
He spins next to me like dense fog.
Only in context do my hands
see how his thumbprints pushed me over,
then underneath the water,
left my childhood stagnant in the pool.
Pushed me so far in,
all I can touch are angels.

Now, like the black and white images
glistening on the TV,
I search, over and over again
for my assassin.

# Annie Frye

I.

Your white hands, withered frighten
though I reach for them with childlike fascination.
Watch how they shake against the blank air,
as if in flight, they might quiver and fall down,
whisper as hands so often do —
enough . . . enough.

I am five, you are nearby 100,
your weathered hands
still able to stir the pot of yams with steel.
A soft voice curls from your tongue,
hums a hymn and you sound like church,
but I can't find the African in your eyes.
Ask my mother a question only a child might muster.
*How can that White woman be my aunt?*
Watch her smile with incredible assurance,
my mother, the darkest of her kin,
hair piled high in a fro, hands extended in a fist,
love beads glistening 'round her shoulders.
I watch her tell me, with no smirk passing from her lips,
that you are black, Annie, dark like coal.

This is when I learn we are the people of rainbow skin.


II.

When I am 13 or so, my mother reveals more of the story.
How you lived with your sister Lillian
in the stone house, loved that White man.
Passed each day in the cobbled streets of 1880,
a Black girl from Virginia faking White skin.

Still faithful in love, I imagine,
one night as your lover stares into your gray eyes,
uncinches the corset, removes the petticoats,
lifts your feet from their tightly laced boots,
that you, the whitest of your kin,

are stripped clean of the lie, as you tell him,
kisses drenching his cheeks,
that your family name is Frye
and Frye means free
for those born Colored but not slave.

After the revelation, he holds you in his watery arms,
and you finally erase that constant fear of pregnancy
and a dark baby shooting out your white thighs . . . .


III.

I will learn much later
when I understand why we wear shackles,
and why we women suffer so,
that Annie never married and her sister
Lillian had one dark child,

named her Grace.

# Integration Part One

In 1969, we move from Philly
to the dream squarely planted in Joppa,
with the big yard and sighs of integration.
With the stares of rednecks,
NIGGER GO HOME,
flags of confederacy waggin' happy to Dixie,
the nearest KKK enclave up the road in Rising Sun.

I learn to keep silent,
grateful for my parents' conviction,
zealots arrived like thirsty men
to the land of milk and honey,
but I am Abraham's child,
almost murdered for god's love,
my parents, unknowingly in cahoots with the devil . . . .

*Every house the same.*
*Every tree planted in the same direction.*

When we move, my mother tells me,
don't let those White kids call you nigger.
Think of James Brown, she says,
I'm Black and I'm proud.
But on the first day of school, I grow quiet,
one hue so loud it tries to melt away all the others.
Young and willing,
I draw pictures of little White girls
with long hair and bangs all day.

An excellent student,
I listen to Barry Manilow and *Stairway to Heaven*.
Straighten my hair.
Speak in a nondescript vernacular.
Learn to smile self-satisfied
when White people tell me
I am not like other little Black girls.

# A Coil Called Skin

for Paul & Randall Robinson

Somewhere deep,
in the back of my DNA,
in that coil called skin,
there is a memory before chains.
But I cannot conjure it.
A story of people naked and satisfied,
their knees anchored in prayer.

By the edge of the Sahara, in the Serengeti,
on the kiss of my lover's tongue,
there is another tale,
a song wrought from steel and revolution.

In these four chambers/in these four corners/in the four walls
of my heart, I spread phoenix wings toward sky,
wrap my wounds in musky soil,
gather tears for you to drown in,
ready myself for the release
of this final reckoning.

As if their melody clings tightly to my womb,
I compose praise songs to Auser and Auset,
Mawu and Lisa. Oludumare.
Anoint my head with Seven Powers.
Stand by Ellegbara
at a cross in the middle of my road.

*But I still can't find heaven here.*

Only yesterday, before this scheme was so
carefully constructed, there was a story I could selfishly
call my own, its words buttressed against the seasons.
It held a legend larger than my life,
a headstone domed in dahlias
to provide solace from the pain.

Once,
these lips held other languages,
my hips were dignified by their size
I knew how to dance with haints and spirits,
anchor these thick dark thighs into the ground,
and grow roots here.

But this is not the good soil,
my handprint everywhere,
but my signature invisible,

and

I cannot remember/ I cannot forget.

Too often when I'm sleeping
I dream a nightmare flowing from earth.
*Thumbs ripped from sockets. Neck locks.*
*Lips pinned to dresses. Backs broken.*
*Heads in rope. Dogs running. Hands bleeding.*

And we wonder why Black folk are crazy.

What happened deep in this soil?

What happened here in America
that made me forget
the story of my name.

I do not know if I am
the Gwa
the Asante
the Igbo
the Yoruba
the Zulu
the Mandinka
the Bena Luluwa, Chockwe, Hutu, Dogon
the Djenne, Banyankolli, Edo, Mbuti
Lomotwa, Xhosa, Wollof,
Fulani, Fon.

I do not know the names of my people,
stripped of everything,
stripped down to the marrow,
to the white crack of bone.

I cry *and* I cry *and* I cry *and* I cry
but I am not Jesus,
and my tears
are neither wide enough

*or* thick enough *or* pure enough
to heal this wound,
to redeem this transgression,

without you.

So I ask that you hold my lack of memory,
sit with the terror of this mourning,
listen without an ounce of denial.

Abide in me and feel the blood staining your toes.
Blood of the Seminole, the Lakota, the Cree.
Blood of Black folk/no tribe.
Blood of Chinese railroad men/Zapatistas.
Blood of Nagasaki/Japanese internment camps.

Blood of body burning on cross.
Body hanging in tree.
Babies bombed in temple.

Blood of no country/no name.
Blood of ignorance.

Each of us swaying to the blue square,
white stars, red.

Walk with me and let our soles change color.

Maybe then
I'll stare into your dark brooding eyes,
our only redemption,
the embrace of hesitant, abundant arms
loving as deeply as we are able.

# Integration Part Two

Later, when I have changed my name,
shaved my head,
made a procession of new found gods,
I grow infatuated with a man who was born like me,
black then white, unhappy,
searching for his color.

Our vernacular peppered with the same struggle,
circa '69.

His voice like autumn weather wooed then chilled,
crisp, then clear, then fading,
like leaves on giant maple trembling with sap,
his skin the faded shade of burlap,
cradling dew-lipped bark,
his eyes sticky, outlining pain.

I fall fast,
like that first leaf that sheds its green for crimson,
tumble willingly into that husk of frightened heartbeats
only to discover the dreads and cowries were only fashion,
the words of love for only friends.

We expired quickly like war's untidy victims,
our bodies melting pots that hide self-loathing,
as we pretend our lovers say nothing about our lives.

We those particular Colored children
turned Black then Afro then African,
breathing demons of integration,
accepted as long we remember White is right,
except of course at the dinner table
where we must recite black-eyed soul with exquisite flavor.
Never be ungrateful.
Nor question existence without a semblance of home.

*Part II: Burning Karma*

# Ulysses

I.

The blood thirst still blisters
despite the smile snatching your cheeks —
fellow warrior feigning amnesia,
your weary tongue stripped of its brilliance
washed clean of battles un/won
and yesterday's prophecies.

Undone by war,
staring at the firing squad with reticence
and regret —

always ready to die.

My disillusioned brother
gone before the bullet strikes
and I'm left to bathe once more
in Yaa Assantewaa's embittered waters,
take up my sword to avenge your death
and the murder of three-year-old boys.

Left to walk the earth alone with my callused tongue,
waiting for my brothers to come home.

The woman remaining
after all the funeral songs have been sung
and the children have been stuffed on fish and rice.

The sistah afraid of midnight for no hands will rock her to sleep.

II.

I need a different vocabulary
for the naming of this rage,
for we are bloodied from the same abandoned journey,
the crimson shrapnel still nestled in our scars.
The chain link dangling from our shoulders.

Like any faithful *omo* of Yemeya,
when I heard my brother screaming, I ran,
carried solace and honey,

why do you only bring your tears?

Remember making Hajj,
trekking Himalayas, laying wreaths at Buddha's feet —
we those dauntless everlasting Fools
discovering ecstasy in a dervish,
then destruction in a kiss.

Old round men smoke our dream in the desert
and we make pinky swears
in our momma's blood.

The same Bodhisattvas
fatigued by heaven's calling and reality's gleam.

Perhaps now ready to quest each other, simply,
as dahlias bloom from seed to sun.
Each petal extended in a long ecstatic moan.

Can't you see the glory of a pomegranate,
its beauty masked in the tasting of 10,000 seeds?

I traversed a world to be here, too.

Won't you stand at the door
and knock —

*Be revealed?*

# Tears for Yashodhara

Like a lotus,
place pain where you can hide it,
delicate behind ears
that understand the language of
falling down,
and getting up again.

Watch you for a moment
silenced in a Bertolucci film.

Wondering how to practice indifference,
while the mascara runs dry.
Cheeks still wet,
from a lover's kiss
and a spiteful, sexless god.

*No vulva ripe with Kali's tongue*
*No womb made ripe with longing.*

Your sorrow unable to supplant
an avatar's bow

as

Siddhartha departs the palace gates
to seek a world's salvation

and you are left
to dispose of the ashes

dutifully.

# Dionysus' Child

Tell me how to craft this prayer Oshun —
how to lay it down right,
so that Gabriel's wings might reach you heavy
with solutions on your mind.

For I can no longer speak my mother tongue,
borne of language only bodies decipher
and poems deconstruct.

How to compose a praise song
to get this black girl some hot love
so she might finally expand her vocabulary
and ponder a different question.

Still obsessed with plump thumbs seared in midnight,
smeared with someone else's DNA.

Goddess who soothes
with honey and sienna hands
lay a veil upon my feet.

Recollect this feeling.

How a storm smells before its arrival,
and leaves peer upward
in preparation for rain.

Don't you remember
laying out the bean cake and mango
the pounded yam and fufu,
the fish, pone, and rice.
Washing deltas with Euphrates and Mississippi waters
then drying scars with lotus buds.
Burning bakhur until like all of Zipporah's daughters
the inside of our thighs tasted of spice.

Recall that sensation
of loving women/laying with men,
black kohl smudged 'gainst your onyx eye,
silk swathed on saffron pillows,

moon warrior running fast
your only sanctum
Yemeya's quiet embers
and swimming with whales

Granddaddy hidden in your first slab of obsidian
momma carved in France
her moist breasts still dripping with milk
eyes still wet with yearning
humming gospel wails as you and Koko inspire man/fits
one more time find yourself at the insane asylum
*tryin' to catch yourself some good lovin' this Saturday night*
*tryin' to catch yourself some good love*
as you lay it down nice and easy
you lay it down sweet
cause nothing can heal you
but this making of babies and baptisms
this conjurin' of swear songs and blues
Oh Lord   Jesus   Hallelujah
causin' a panic by the front door
hoping this month
your fingertips are splashed to red

Recollect this feeling
when I pray
*ye ye ye ye oh*
and warrant some divine intervention.

For Zeus will not come
and Hera is raging.

# Waking to Wound

Never kissed to marrow,
I burn toward middle age deceived.
No crash or blush or tremor,
washes this desire down
to something palpable and discreet.
I finger tit until the nipple pops to tear.
Only imaginary lovers scratch my womb,
thumb nightmares, so that now,
I entertain celibacy as a certain kind of normal.

I wake to wound, early morning.
Watch the spirits flicker in the hazy night/day.
The street lamp, humming its constant buzz,
undresses my scars.

Alone grief stings hotter than any sarcasm
that might slip off my tongue in daybreak,
as I wonder what brave soul
might dip his fingers into this sticky pot,
climb the hedge, break through the windows to see
I am more than some prickly barricade.

The morning shadow slips from shade to light to color.
Who will raise their eye toward chasm
first with lip, then belly, then sigh . . . .

# the pickup

all conversation now lingers
toward that common denominator —
bodies woven decisively
against the longitude of a 2 a.m. possibility

the eyes are bloodshot, but well,
the fatigue illuminates their gleam,
makes them look almost shiny,
next to the pearl of your
bloodshot eyes

flushed

I imagine you have the power
to make me quiver
as knees collapse
into the thralls of uncompromising propositions

but soon you'll be like all the other part-time loves
your caprice exchanged for wartime maneuvers
calisthenics, executed dimly in the corners
of my full size bed

outside the bar,
harsh lights reveal nothing clandestine
under the hardened lashes and unfurled lip
except a faded cloak of night
masquerading as morning

but I've succumbed to a woman's prerogative
and need to suck a succulent lie 'tween my teeth

tonight

while all the lights in B-more are closing
and I am shutting down the bars

beneath the street lamps
you ramble incessantly
about the chiaroscuro of black girl's soul
knowing full well you have never tasted darker berries

and who knows —
maybe these pomes have lost their flavor
their sweetness permanently eroded by fools like you
but tonight I pretend that even children
can decipher the postmodern metaphors
encrypted in the neon signs

yes, I understand as we start waving down the cabs
there will be no making of affection here
but we can fuck, right
our bodies woven,
but never tied to anything beyond idle sweat

and

maybe if I had an ounce of sense
I'd learn to run girl run
or wait for the bus
or a possible A train going in any direction,
but yours
but, well, it's 2 a.m. and it's been a long time since
anyone made that particular proposition

so I squint hard to make you beautiful
against the beacon of a Saab
going round the curb

I can make believe you anything
against the shadow and the light

even pretend my silence masks a moan

# Drinking Coffee

Rocking me back to the soft pangs of want,
I stare at the man planting
the one cowry shell in his hair.
Suffocating . . . .

We sit in the cafe. My hands shake.
Feeling grows like a noose to understanding,
desire planted as squarely as the fear.

He use to wear a string of cowries,
holy vulvas propped keenly
against his collarbone
as if to correct the demons of his sex.

Then suddenly the necklace went away
and he replaced it with a metal chain,
but there are no quick steps for fashioning soul.

I think, as we drink the coffee,
sit at the table we so often frequent,
I might want to climb in,
have the man shut his mouth,
and listen to the message of one heartbeat,
then two.

As I drive to the cafe,
a truck with the license plate *Ulysses*
passes my car,

the name foretelling,
as the man tries to woo with tears,
plant the shell with provocation.
His eyes, already red, midmorning, will stare,
struggling for meaning
as I pour the cream into the brown,
listen, like the famished, to stories of my wonder,
*(but not quite wonderful enough),*

and remember that first time touching,
fingered light echoing love through a telephone wire.
How my voice, firmly nestled against indifference,
would slowly melt to honey croon,
so that when we finally met,
I wore makeup for the first time in years.
Felt god open a door
and make a covenant with my desire.

Later I would curse her as a selfish prick,
as any man, a whore,
as I watched my love poured into another,
my titties shamefully suckled in the tender wood,

just like massa,
his ennui redeemed by the black coffee.

# Requiem
## for Kathie

I.

I kneel before the confessional. Knees scarred.
There is no priest. I am the only executioner.
Remember what the friend says when we speak of love,

*what is known is known in the mode of the object.*

We have found one another after a long eclipse,
sisters falling in and out of love.
The feeling, much like watching your child burst into womanhood.
You stare awkward, then amazed.
Kisses grow sweet with time,
as frightened voices cling weekly to the wire,
and we glimpse Death's angel by the backdoor,
Az'rael's darting wings daring us to change life's course,
as we carry others, untimely to grave, our bodies older,
holding life like a concealed weapon,
love's initiates shaking at the grail,
each heart broken in the same chamber,
changed.

Your name always interrupting,
after the friend and I have dismantled
the epistemology of longing.

You, the man who is constantly coming,
but who will not arrive.


II.

Spring has gone unnoticed.
The bulb heads of purpled crocus
splattered in soon to be graves.
The yellow of daffodils is dull,
and even tulips cannot flirt with me,
their heads tilting left, then right
with indignation.

Birds fly 'round my head and I am a waiting room.

Climb into a dying friend's bed,
squeeze resistance like only fleshy bodies can,
with cold kisses and bribe-filled prayers,
desperate for one last battle cry from her
honey-speckled voice,
and to quench my need
to be seen,
if not by millions of men,
at least one,
who might cherish this blood red dahlia —
huge, coveted, and possibly
too beautiful for this world.


III.

Once the man told me,
I see the cream inside that cage,
and poof —
he worked so hard to find the key
its whereabouts mapped in kindness
and simple prayers
muttered with two mouths.

I loved him despite myself,
despite a dead friend's warnings,
as he appealed to the deadliest of all my sins,
the vanity of my spirit,
and waited, like the rabid,
for my heart's true utterance,
only to remark, *oh no*,
as I endured another kind of dying
a man's gaze no longer petal soft
loathsome hands
snatching me to Hades,
his brided eunuch,
proclaimed trivial
like a forget-me-not or a rose.

IV.

In dreams I wake with the man parting my tongue —
our earthly argument has made a battlefield of heaven.

The magenta cloth draping my bedroom
burns then clouds my vision,
in the nightmares he peels back my skin.
I unzip him,
then make a five pointed star with his fear,
the sex always language rather than pleasure,
and he can never decipher the code.

Fantasy ever hungry for a word, simply spread
across my lips, like a hand across my thoughts,
as he urges (in that way only men can)
*open wider please*
and my needy thighs shiver,
then tighten against a friend's good advice —
*nothing that a coward plants,*
*will ever bloom a seed.*

# Poem for a Black Man
# I Once Loved

Your eyes have seen too much death,
like other brothers, you hide their wounds,
then wonder why I bring no salve.

Black man, eyes wrinkled,
they grow small
buried in the triplets   sister mother   friends
you have carried to grave.
Better understanding,
like age, settles in my bones,
and I will write no more blood poems
etched in your name.
Only wonder why our skins can touch,
but never meet when we make love.

Unglued in your eyes,
I tumble underneath their years,
with bold stares,
ask their lessons to unbuckle my skin.
Your body, soft like a woman's,
rides the wet, musky rhythm,
cardamom-filled,
like the pot of tea I will linger against
upon your departure.

Language measured hesitation
next to the broken bed,
staining sheets with impressions
that will not cleanse away our sins,
as hands break cycles,
then moisten the pattern
with the same wound.

I stare into your eyes.   *You wobble.*

Tenderly close your lids against my hands,
eyes so buried in, I can hardly see them
except to push against your temples,
lift for a moment,
the sparkle from your dark orbs,
let it spackle my skin with temporary salvation
as history appoints
another sad story
indelibly into motion.

# Mandala

## for Bruce

Everywhere, I see the pattern.
In dying leaf mulched to earth,
near anthill wrestled to dust,
underneath the porcelain tears
shuddering on my daughter's lash.
All the same. Forever changing.
Except on those rare occasions
when the sand is strewn in a familiar direction,
and I am frightened by the resemblance
of yesterday's glow,

for I have tasted this specific point in space before,
and did not care for its offerings,
concealed wound,
whispering past me like a hungry succubus
as memory sweeps your hair to forehead,
and I slumber inside those thick arms
that have forsworn all women.

*So young.*

*So young.*

The summer the lama warned —
children split from the same cloth
always come unwound by the same thread,
as we pressed our patterns tighter,
the braided woman and ex-priest,
hesitantly shaking underneath newborn raptures,
causing blasphemies, for there is no language
to describe this love without offending.
Someone.

Inscribing homilies in your hands
as we walked through St. Matthew's
and I swore the frescoes knew we were holy,
the clamor of our voices so familiar
we would call the laughter our first time.

Now in chase of that young girl
who dwelled in the garden,
unable to shift my gaze in wonder,
but desperate for that flush of love again,
my bed full of dead men wrapped in crimson sheets,
a new one freshly laid in the sarcophagus,
as I can find no words to slay you,
loved once beyond the husk.

I, a monk weaving the mandala,
only to destroy it with one stroke,
my ancient voice, old, then young, then neither.

*Look*, she whispers,
taking up the knife
and marking a new pattern,
*how beautiful you are,*
*to have trusted love so completely,*
*once.*

# moonkissed

the lover quakes
as the moon parts her thighs with similar caverns —
her moan low and husky,
as the earth, grating on its axis
bellows a lamentation
and a sigh

cedar lutes crushed by Pan float against parched lips,
and in the timbre of wood songs
she no longer recognizes
the sound that once called her forth,
bloody to the world

a moody saffron light drifts from the kitchen
with the taste of cinnamon lilting on its tongue

the woman lingers in a familiar feeling

her beloved so close the scent of sandalwood and lime
leaves a cloying remembrance of footprints

sure he is just stumbling down the road
wandering drunk past trees and naked palms
searching for a metaphor that might snatch his tongue
and make it true in the moon's presence

staring at the sky
she makes up new patterns
for the stars' arrangement,
names a constellation for her weary traveler,

so close she feels his sandals clutching the earth
the distance unbearable

so close,
that when she shuts her eyes,
his stare back into the dark awakening
and trembling cup of wine

# The Glance

Oh, I am ruined now. Happy day.
Feet move unsteadily on the path —
for once, I cannot contrive
what direction might relieve this ache.

I lie in bed, eyes squeezed tight,
try to cleave to your image,
but memory never grabs your essence
as clearly as my eyes. Even photographs
will not suffice, for in your face, I am mostly
transfixed by the small veins seeking refuge.

The next time we talk, let the hours weave our words
into a coarse-skinned blanket, you will take your glasses off,
I will fall into your caverns —
count how many blood-filled lines cross your retinas.

Shed no tear,
as I note how many cracked vessels I find . . . .

Pretend the smile hanging against your lips
is not some sublime thief bent on your self destruction,
but rather a gift, and in gratitude (or perhaps fear),
I will feign ignorance to all your pain, hope, one day
you might trust this woman with the truth of your sorrow.

Who until yesterday, did not believe
she could ever be hushed into a shy goodbye again —
now desperate to cram all this feeling
into a gesture you might understand,
as I fumble toward love, awkwardly,
find her huddled in the dust balls lurking behind the piano,
or dancing in the curry smoldering on the stove.

Look, there's even some honeyed wood charred in the burner.

Now my daughter glares with the defiant eyes of a worried mother
as I gaze upward, mesmerized by the bright light
shooting holes through the bamboo shades,

and though choice may be my only guide,
when you and I are together
it is as if I have always known you,
and everything —
even the disappointments
that claimed my youth and the sweetness of this tongue,
become part of some greater mystery all divined to bring us together,
for god in her infinite wisdom
did keep my innocence alive . . . .

If only for this short embrace
and inevitable glance.

# Burning Karma

Naive, I met the Buddha on the road,
only to discover recognition's fate.
I killed him, yet before the slaying,
let the snake swallow me in one grand gesture
like a python, whole.

In his garden he digested me for years,
I watched him secretly smile under the apple tree,
yet he was much like Peter,
afraid of the dark seed unraveled in our sitting.

He denied me often.

I died in that deep snake belly, only to be remade,
a torrent of petals, near bloom,
hands hot in the center, cobbled with knowing eye.
Neither Satan nor Adam
able to build a temple to my insignificance,
as I scour the earth woman,
condemned to hemorrhage wiser.

Remember love so potent, I called it holy,
grew tipsy upon its embrace,
crawled inside a snake, instead of self,
renamed my dream obsession,

and like the reed, broken once, then twice,
and on its third severing,
anchors itself firmly, yet forever crooked in the marsh,
I watch the ribbon that once bound us
flame in the orange glow of afterlight,
the man coiled in his closet,
waiting for a cock to crow
as he secretly thumbs the ash.

# what a smooth Taoist brother intimated before kissing

for Ken

sweet sister
do not believe me Solomon
for I find you more than comely and dark
ancient ember of Makeda
dancing in Soledad and Roanoke
moaning Gullah cries for the Bantu

wield your machete

I'll embrace warrior tears
discover what sits beside
your untouchable sorrows
the wounds forever etched beneath your
broken blade of lash

and unlike other menfolk
let you carve mandalas
meticulously into skin

for I will hold you
even when Death comes a knockin'
be that haint forever dancin' round
your porch light,
dissatisfied you don't come 'round much
anymore

so let me carve this kiss
indelibly at memory's doorway and
divine my path toward home

I'll love all those black girl scars
love 'em real good 'til they weep
and we make new skin together
the course of your neck
10,000 tribulations drawing us on

my ebony cloud burning —
I'll bring the rain today
make water inside your
rounded thigh and raven lip
this serpent swaying in your loving, capable arms
tenderly untwisting
the scarlet ribbons buried
between your temples

my head upon your sickle
body thrust into the flame
limbs enraptured upon Kali's pillow
content

grateful I can take what is offered
knowing your chasm will never be filled

primal sistah
even in death,
I'll come knockin'

be that moth abuzzin'
toward the brilliance —
forever smooching in your ears

# Coda

A January cyclone ignites his ghost again.
Lifts me from my feet. Surprise.
I did not see these tears coming.
Light snow sprinkled on pavement,
my prayer a hot thrash toward heaven,
hearty this time, a rant, or *revelio* against gray sky.
I want to make him dead, but his prickly thumbs
keep tapping my hatred. At least god,
make him a quiet hush of wind. I could survive that,
but he is like a pitchfork these days
digging, then shuffling me back into the ground.
Please, do not make this one a heavy breeze
that can pry open even the earth.

Ten years to peel a man's soul from a woman's.
That's what the Taoists say.
Once inside, his essence stains like semen,
lingers in every taste, you smell him in your bones
find his shadow-filled slippers curled beside the bed,
a greedy incubus knotting your dream.

Be careful who enters your jade gate.

You women know of what I speak.

Cups too often gripping sentiment
until it evaporates to half life.

# Stillness
# September 10, 2001

There is a beauty that comes
when the world, despite her rage
smiles at you with the might of a
soul embrace. When time is
measured in the width of a heartbeat
and an ache that demands no peace.

It's when you feel the presence
and her ever faithful footprints
renaming sky.

When you have nothing to move
but the quivering of yourself.

# Passport for the Recently Dead

At first there is a light unnamable
like original thought,
you will not understand its meaning,
but it will be familiar like that first tear
that hurled you from the belly of a lonely soul
into the world.

The light will point,
counter to all your instinct,
toward a destination tunneled in REM.
Surprised by Death,
you will tumble until the inside is out.

One day old, the light will fashion
another playground, as the angels weep
well done,

and loved ones search your meat body for air,
Death stealing kisses,
only to rake them in rapture.

Don't be frightened
when those earthbound rituals
try to excavate your dream.

The living will be home soon —
the conjuring of the dead
always and forever a loud shout.

# About the Author

A dramatist and actor as well as a poet, Kumani (Denise Gantt) has been an Artist-in-Residence at the Maryland Institute College of Art and worked with the Rebecca Project for Human Rights, an arts and advocacy program for women in drug recovery. For many years she was the director of Theater for a New Generation, Center Stage's outreach and education program. She has performed in play readings directed by Tony Kushner and Danny Hoch, and has read her poetry at the Kennedy Center, Villa Julie College, Living Stage, Baltimore Women's Detention Center, the Maryland Institute College of Art, the Creative Alliance, the Learning Center, Center Stage, and Joe's Movement Emporium. *conjuring the dead* is her first full length collection of poems.

# Acknowledgements

On behalf of the Literary Arts at Artscape, the Baltimore Festival of the Arts would like to acknowledge and thank Mayor Martin O'Malley; the Maryland State Arts Council; Sam Schmidt of WordHouse for his ideas and enthusiasm; WordHouse Press and the Baltimore Writers' Alliance; Barbara Simon, President, Maryland State Poetry & Literary Society; Robin Green-Cary, Owner, Sibanye; Maryland Emerging Voices Competition judges Afaa Michael Weaver, Lia Purpura and Mimi Zannino; and artist Sam Christian Holmes. This book and the Maryland Emerging Voices Award are administered by The Baltimore Office of Promotion & The Arts.

# Author's Acknowledgements

To Estelle and David Gantt, Maya Yasmeen Gantt, David Gantt, Jr., Kathie Narcizo, Christie Polan-Bonitz, Johnnett Kent, Ellie Robinson, Marlene Cooper, Polly Riddims, StrongHeart, Jaan Whitehead, Lisa Biggs, Tanisha Brady-Christie, Lauren Fitzgerald, Lakia Green, Vanessa Thomas, Malika Saada Saar, Imani Walker, and my tormentors who I have renamed teacher, thank you for nurturing this poet's journey with your lessons, love, and tears.

To Hedgebrook and Norcroft writer's retreats, immeasurable gratitude for helping me to unleash my dark woman voice in your beautiful surroundings.

To my Egungun, the dead, thank you for gracing this work with your stories of pain, struggle, and vast joy.

To the Divine Mystery, thank you for making a way.